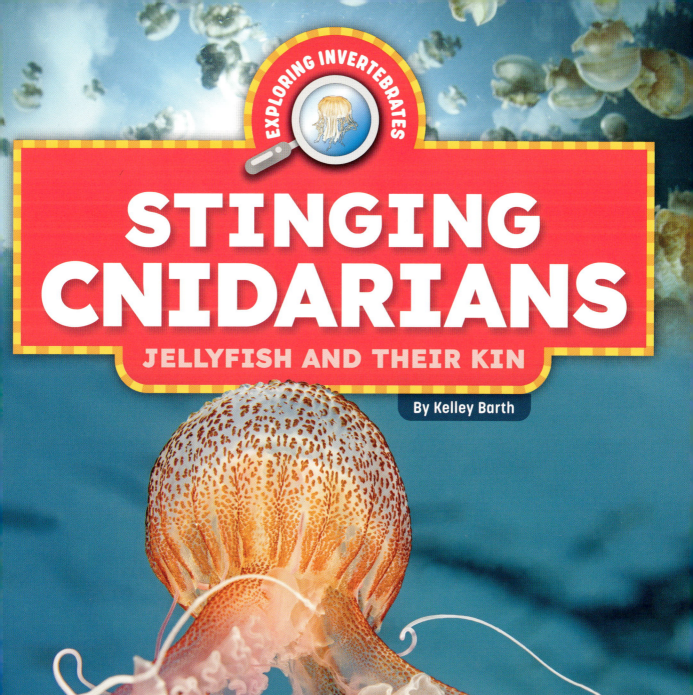

Exploring Invertebrates

STINGING CNIDARIANS
JELLYFISH AND THEIR KIN

By Kelley Barth

childsworld.com

Published by The Child's World®
800-599-READ • childsworld.com

Copyright © 2025 by The Child's World®
All rights reserved. No part of this book may be reproduced or utilized in any form or by any means without written permission from the publisher.

Photography Credits
Cover: ©Erik Isselee/Shutterstock; Ethan Daniels/Shutterstock; Gerard Soury/The Image Bank/Getty Images; page 3: ©divedog/Shutterstock; page 4: ©lokesh164/Shutterstock; pages 4–5; 24: Bernatskaia Oksana/Shutterstock; page 5: ©irin-k/Shutterstock; page 5: ©prapat1120/Shutterstock; pages 5, 12: ©1st-ArtZone/Shutterstock; page 5: ©Sebastian Kaulitzski/Shutterstock; soft_light/Shutterstock; pages 6–7: ©Stephen Frink/The Image Bank/Shutterstock; page 8: ©g images.com/Shutterstock; page 9: ©Paul Starosta/Stone/Getty Images; ©Allexxandar/Shutterstock; pages 10–11: ©Ai Angel Gentel/Moment/Getty Images; page 13: ©VectorMine/Shutterstock; ©H. Tanaka/Shutterstock; page 14–15: ©Giordano Cipriani/The Image Bank/Getty Images; page 16: ©Eric Isselee/Shutterstock; ©Marti Bug Catcher/Shutterstock; page 17: ©Rebecca Schreiner/Shutterstock; ©Romolo Tavani/Shutterstock: page 18–19: ©Gerard Soury/The Image Bank/Getty Images; page 20: ©H. Tanaka/Shutterstock; page 21: ©g images.com/Shutterstock; page 22: ©Lori Bye

ISBN Information
9781503894532 (Reinforced Library Binding)
9781503894754 (Portable Document Format)
9781503895577 (Online Multi-user eBook)
9781503896390 (Electronic Publication)

LCCN
2024941363

Printed in the United States of America

ABOUT THE AUTHOR

Kelley Barth is a former children's librarian who loves connecting with young people over stories and books. When she isn't busy writing, she enjoys reading, hiking, crafting, and going on adventures with her husband and son.

CONTENTS

CHAPTER 1
MEET THE CNIDARIAN . . . 4

CHAPTER 2
CNIDARIAN BODIES . . . 8

CHAPTER 3
THE LIFE CYCLE OF A CNIDARIAN . . . 12

CHAPTER 4
CNIDARIANS IN THE WORLD . . . 19

CHAPTER 5
THE FUTURE OF CNIDARIANS . . . 20

Wonder More . . . 21
Floating Jellyfish . . . 22
Glossary . . . 23
Find Out More . . . 24
Index . . . 24

CHAPTER 1

MEET THE CNIDARIAN

A swimmer paddles into the warm, salty ocean. They peek underneath the water. The ocean is busy and full of life. Thousands of corals dot the ocean floor. Together they make up a coral reef.

The swimmer keeps a safe distance. Next to the coral is a colorful sea anemone. Its **tentacles** are floating in the water, searching for food. But wait! Something is floating in the distance. A jellyfish is coming. The swimmer moves away. They know not to touch the creature or get too close. All three of these animals are cnidarians (ny-DAYR-ee-uhns)—and cnidarians sting.

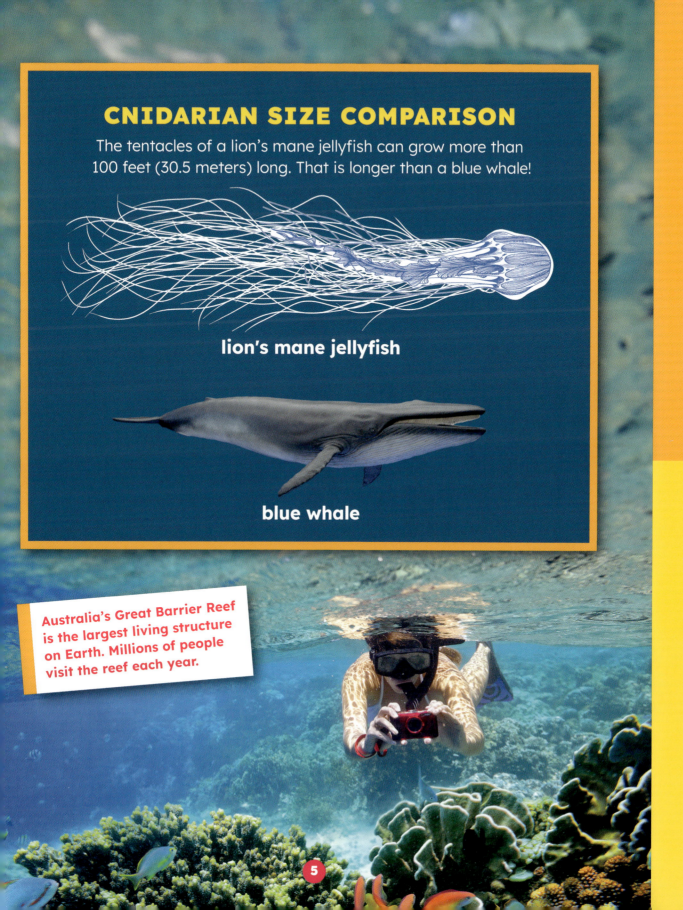

CNIDARIAN SIZE COMPARISON

The tentacles of a lion's mane jellyfish can grow more than 100 feet (30.5 meters) long. That is longer than a blue whale!

lion's mane jellyfish

blue whale

Australia's Great Barrier Reef is the largest living structure on Earth. Millions of people visit the reef each year.

A Portuguese man o' war's tentacles can be up to 165 feet (50 meters) long.

Cnidarians are a type of **invertebrate**. They live in every ocean in the world. A few even live in freshwater lakes or streams. Corals live in shallow salt water. They need sunlight to grow. Some sea anemones live deep on the ocean floor. A few cnidarians live in cold water. But most are found in warm water.

Cnidarians have different ways of moving around—that is, if they move around at all! Corals don't move. They attach to rocks and stay put. Sea anemones usually stay put, too. But they can move slowly on their base. They usually move when they feel threatened or to find food. Most jellyfish don't really swim. They are carried by ocean **currents** and float long distances. Box jellyfish are built differently. They are strong swimmers.

CHAPTER 2

CNIDARIAN BODIES

Cnidarians are different shapes, sizes, and colors. They don't have bones, a brain, a heart, or lungs. Cnidarians have **radial symmetry**. This means their bodies are shaped like a circle around a central point. Think about a bicycle wheel or a pizza. These have radial symmetry, just like cnidarians.

Cnidarians don't have a head. But they do have a mouth. Their mouth helps them eat and get rid of waste. Cnidarians also have tentacles. But be careful—the tentacles sting!

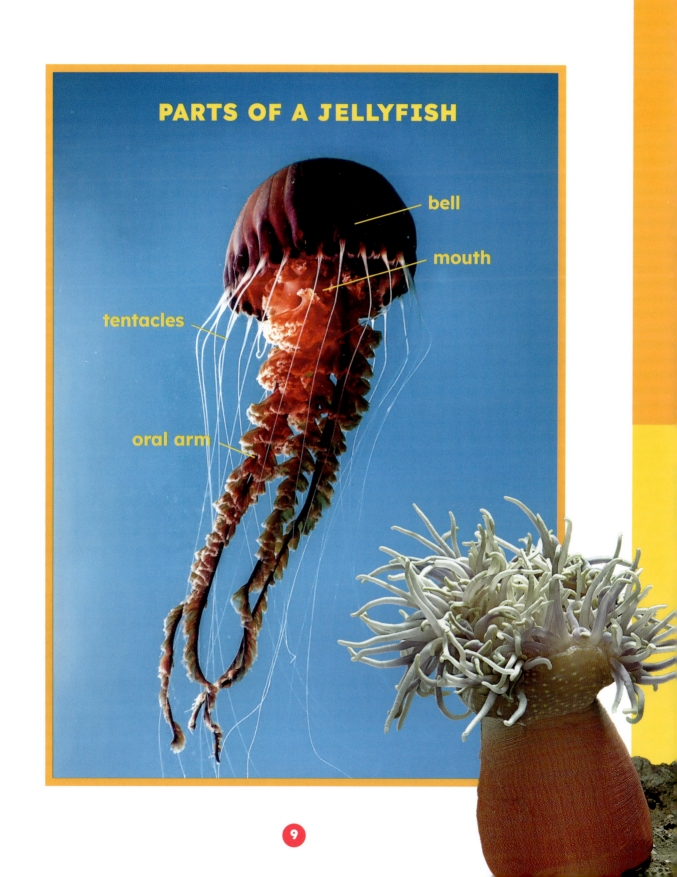

WATCH OUT FOR STINGS!

Jellyfish tentacles can release venom even after the animal dies. Be careful if you see a jellyfish washed up on the beach! They can still give a painful sting. There is a myth that says if you get stung by a jellyfish, you should put urine on the sting to help the pain. This is not true. Urine can make a jellyfish sting even worse.

Jellyfish and other squishy invertebrates are the main food group for leatherback sea turtles. These turtles are known as gelatinivores, which means they only eat things that are jelly-like.

Cnidarians have stinging cells on their tentacles. They use these stingers to help catch their food. The stingers shoot **venom** into other animals that come too close. Venom **paralyzes** the animals so they can't move. Then, it's dinnertime. Cnidarians are carnivores. This means they eat other animals. They mostly eat fish and tiny creatures called plankton.

Some cnidarian stings don't hurt humans. They might just cause a small rash. But other stings can be very painful. Some are even deadly. The box jellyfish is one of the most dangerous animals in the world.

CHAPTER 3
THE LIFE CYCLE OF A CNIDARIAN

Cnidarians can have one of two body types. **Polyp** bodies are shaped like tubes with a mouth on top. They have tentacles facing upward around their mouth. Coral and sea anemones are polyp-shaped.

Medusa bodies are shaped like an umbrella or a bell. Their mouth and tentacles hang downward. Jellyfish start with a polyp shape and grow into a medusa.

Cnidarians often start as eggs. Eggs grow into **larvae** and then become adults. But many polyps have another way of growing. New buds often grow on coral. These buds can break off and become their own coral. Other polyp animals can even **clone** themselves.

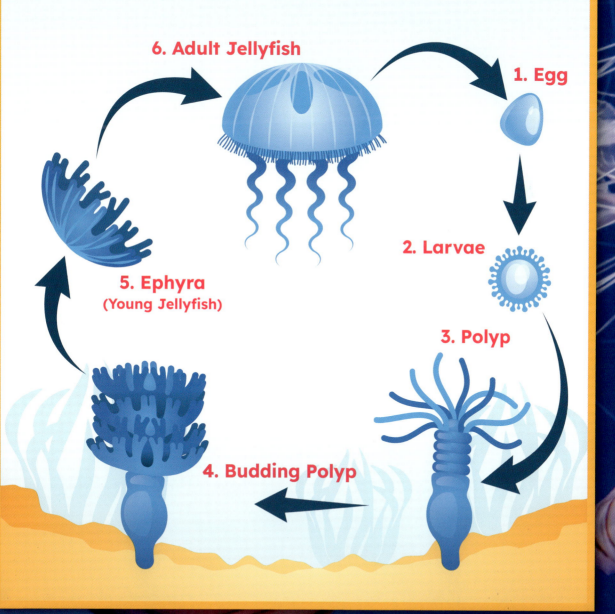

Anemones protect clownfish from fish that want to eat them. Clownfish scare away other fish that threaten the anemones.

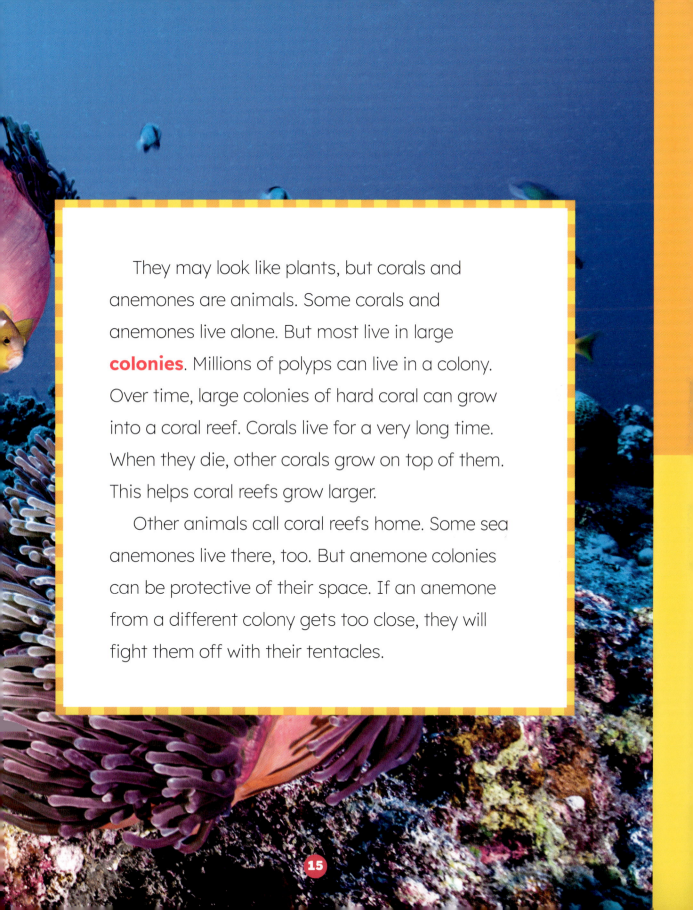

They may look like plants, but corals and anemones are animals. Some corals and anemones live alone. But most live in large **colonies**. Millions of polyps can live in a colony. Over time, large colonies of hard coral can grow into a coral reef. Corals live for a very long time. When they die, other corals grow on top of them. This helps coral reefs grow larger.

Other animals call coral reefs home. Some sea anemones live there, too. But anemone colonies can be protective of their space. If an anemone from a different colony gets too close, they will fight them off with their tentacles.

Medusa cnidarians include box jellyfish, Portuguese man-of-wars, and many other kinds of jellyfish. Many of these animals are known for their beauty. They come in all sizes and colors. But it can be hard to spot a jellyfish. Many of them are see-through. Others light up and glow in the dark ocean!

Most medusas don't live long. Some live only a few months. But the immortal jellyfish lives much longer. In fact, they might live forever! When this medusa is injured or starving, it doesn't die. Instead, it turns back into its polyp stage and starts its life cycle all over again. There is still so much we have to learn about these animals.

SNAKES ALIVE!

Medusa is a character from Greek mythology. She was a monster who could turn people to stone just by looking at them. Her hair was made of snakes. They looked like the tentacles of a jellyfish. This is why jellyfish bodies are called medusa.

Some jellyfish have hundreds of tentacles, while others have just a few.

Small anemones attached to this crab's shell create a living suit of armor that protects the crab from predators.

CHAPTER 4

CNIDARIANS IN THE WORLD

When two different types of animals help each other, it is called **symbiosis**. Many cnidarians use symbiosis. Most animals avoid sea anemones because of their sting. But clownfish live in an anemone's tentacles. A special slimy coating on their bodies helps keep clownfish from being stung. This is helpful for both animals. Clownfish stay safe from **predators**. Anemones eat waste from the clownfish.

Cnidarians have symbiosis with many other ocean animals. Algae often live in corals. It gives corals food and oxygen. In turn, the corals keep the algae safe. Some small anemones live on top of crab shells. Other fish live safely within jellyfish tentacles. Cnidarians play an important role in the ocean.

CHAPTER 5

THE FUTURE OF CNIDARIANS

Earth's oceans are getting warmer. This has a big impact on cnidarians. A group of jellyfish is called a bloom. Most jellyfish blooms prefer living in warm water. As the oceans get warmer, blooms often grow larger. They take over areas of the ocean and harm the other animals that live there. Changes to the environment are also harmful to corals. When ocean water becomes too warm, they die.

These changes cause problems for other ocean animals. They can also make it difficult for humans who want to enjoy the ocean. Scientists are still learning how our changing oceans will impact cnidarians in the future.

WONDER MORE

Wondering About New Information

What did you learn about cnidarians? Write down three new facts you learned. Did this information surprise you? Why or why not?

Wondering How It Matters

Cnidarians are affected by the health of their environment. What are some ways your environment affects you? How do you affect your environment? What are some ways you could help ocean environments and cnidarians?

Wondering Why

Cnidarians are known for their stings. What are some of the ways their stingers help cnidarians? What other animals can sting? How does stinging help them?

Ways to Keep Wondering

After reading this book, what questions do you have about cnidarians? What can you do to learn more about them?

FLOATING JELLYFISH

Make your own jellyfish, or even an entire bloom if you'd like. Use your imagination. There are so many different types of jellyfish!

Steps to Take

1) Color one coffee filter with markers. This will be the "bell" of your jellyfish.

2) Spray the coffee filter with water and watch the jelly's color spread!

3) Let the coffee filter dry.

4) Start adding ribbon, yarn, or other materials along the underside of the jellyfish for the tentacles. Attach with a stapler. Make sure to use a different material or color for the jellyfish's oral arms. They need both types!

5) Tie a string through the top of your jellyfish and hang them up.

6) Enjoy your beautiful creation. But watch out for stings!

Supplies
- coffee filters
- washable markers
- a spray bottle filled with water
- string or ribbon
- assorted yarn, crepe paper, ribbons, etc.
- stapler

GLOSSARY

clone (KLOHN) To clone is to create an exact copy of a living thing.

colonies (KOL-uh-neez) Colonies are groups of animals that all live together in one area.

currents (KUR-ents) Currents are the direction of movement of large bodies of water.

invertebrate (in-VUR-tuh-bruht) An invertebrate is an animal that does not have a spine.

larvae (LAR-vee) Larvae are the early form of an animal before they change into an adult.

medusa (muh-DOO-suh) A medusa is an animal with a body shaped like a bell, like jellyfish.

paralyze (PAYR-uh-lyze) Paralyze means to make an animal unable to move.

polyp (PAH-lip) A polyp is an animal with a tubelike body that has a mouth and tentacles on one end, like corals or sea anemones.

predators (PRED-uh-turz) Predators are animals that live by hunting other animals for food.

radial symmetry (RAY-dee-uhl SIM-uh-tree) Radial symmetry is when an animal's body parts are arranged in a balanced way around a center point.

symbiosis (sim-bee-OH-suhs) Symbiosis is when two different animals have a cooperative relationship.

tentacles (TEN-tuh-kulz) Tentacles are long flexible armlike structures that help an animal feel or grasp.

venom (VEH-num) Venom is poison that one animal injects into another.

FIND OUT MORE

In the Library

Culliford, Amy. *Jellyfish*. Coral Springs, FL: Seahorse Publishing, 2022.

Spencer, Erin. *The World of Coral Reefs*. North Adam, MA: Storey Publishing, 2022.

Zimmerman, Adline J. *Sea Anemones*. Minneapolis, MN: Jump!, 2022.

On the Web

Visit our website for links about cnidarians:
childsworld.com/links

Note to Parents, Caregivers, Teachers, and Librarians: We routinely verify our web links to make sure they are safe and active sites. So encourage your readers to check them out!

INDEX

anemone, 4, 7, 12, 14–15, 18–19

coral, 7, 12, 15, 19–20

jellyfish, 4–5, 7, 9–13, 16–17, 19–20

medusa, 12, 16–17

polyp, 12–13, 15–16

radial symmetry, 8

stingers, 11, 21
symbiosis, 19

tentacle, 4–6, 8–12, 15, 17, 19

venom, 10–11